I0476312

Moving Up the Nonprofit Ladder:

Success Strategies for Women.

John Yowell
Richard Hoefer

The Center for Advocacy, Nonprofit and Donor Organizations (CAN-DO)
University of Texas at Arlington School of Social Work
211 S. Cooper Street • PO Box 19129 Arlington, TX 76019

Find us online at www.uta.edu/can-do

Prologue

Hello. Welcome to Moving Up the Nonprofit Ladder: Success Strategies for Women. This brief report, put together by the UTA Center for Advocacy, Nonprofit, and Donor Organizations (CAN-DO) is meant to help female professionals in the nonprofit sector take their careers to the next level; that of leadership or executive positions within their organization. Additionally, we hope that this book is useful to existing organizational leaders to demonstrate to them that their agencies need women in these positions to fully realize their potential and fulfill their mission.

As a woman in the nonprofit sector you no doubt have seen the dramatic disparity that exists between the roles men and women are given in many organizations. If you work for a large agency, it is likely that your board of directors and top management positions are almost entirely filled with men despite the overwhelming majority of women engaged in doing the work on the ground. In fact, this is the case with many industries, nonprofit or otherwise, in which women make up the majority of the workforce; teachers, nurses, retail, the list goes on. Now at first, you might be tempted to chalk this up to the priorities of men vs. women. In putting this report together we've seen articles and research make such claims over and over. Men are competitive and money-driven. They desire to lead while women are focused on interpersonal connections, balancing work and family, and working directly with clients.

Despite these perceptions, nonprofits with women at the helm consistently outperform their male-led counterparts in many measures, and they do so, it appears, without having to compromise their values. Instead, women incorporate their empathy and interpersonal skills into their leadership roles. Our interpretation of the literature is that the only trait that really makes a difference is access. The real reason that men are in leadership positions more than women is because they have far greater access. Men simply have the open access to leadership positions because they have always had it. Engrained pathways, "The Old Boys Club," preferential hiring practices; whatever labels we choose to place on the systemic issues of gender discrimination, women are still fighting for equal access, equal pay, and the kind of direct path to leadership that men have enjoyed for quite a long time. This report gives you, the female nonprofit professional, the added firepower necessary to take to this fight and emerge victorious.

Beyond the hypothetical, theoretical, and more idealistic discussions, this report will also give you the practical steps necessary to begin your journey to leadership immediately. These steps will help you prioritize your career goals and then, as your plans dictate, begin to set yourself apart within your organization as someone who wants to lead; someone who is an asset to the future of your agency. You will learn how to connect with the board of directors, a critical component of moving to top positions. We will also help you analyze your current position in the new light of your motivation to advance and show you how to make your agency's success your success by engaging in your organization's mission outside of the office. Finally we will discuss how, as an emerging leader, you can work to facilitate larger change within the industry in order to ease the struggle for advancement for the next generation of female nonprofit leaders.

Section I:

The Current Situation

For decades the nonprofit sector's ranks have been dominated by women. Yet the vast majority of these women find themselves and their careers inhibited by the same glass ceiling that is so pervasive in the corporate world. Just as in the for profit sector, women are dramatically underrepresented in leadership roles, especially within larger organizations where engrained pathways to upper management and executive positions both favor and are dominated by men. Moreover, where women do find upper level executive work in the nonprofit sector they can expect to earn significantly less, by more than 30% in some subsectors, than their male counterparts. Furthermore, despite some progress in the for-profit sector in this area, the nonprofit income gap appears to be growing. According to data from 2014, this income gap is especially pronounced in organizations with operating budgets of less than $500,000. Among these agencies the annual wage-gap ranged from around $2,500 to more than $30,000 depending on the type of position the agency's financial situation. All of this in a sector in which there already exists a lower overall salary for entry level and non-management positions and an uncertain level of job security as funding for small and mid-level organizations diminishes under economic and political pressures.

These facts are more than a little disturbing given that the nonprofit sector is itself designed to serve disenfranchised populations such as women, children, racial and ethnic minorities, impoverished peoples, oppressed religious groups, and any number of other groups who struggle under the weight of innumerable institutions from which they find themselves alienated. The status quo is also quite frustrating considering the fact that nonprofit organizations with larger proportions of women in leadership roles have been demonstrated to be more effective in their missions, have higher employee satisfaction and lower employee turnover, are more effective in fundraising, and employ a more democratic and participatory style of leadership which is well-suited to the ethos of the nonprofit sector. Research has further shown that organizations with more female board members are more likely to report satisfaction with board performance. They are also better equipped to reach out to and establish a reliable female donor and volunteer base.

Despite all of these issues, women continue to be drawn to the nonprofit sector for many reasons. Nonprofits tend to be more willing to work with their schedule thus allowing them to more easily balance family and work, a benefit especially important to young or single parents. There is also an abundance of opportunity for women in nonprofit organizations. Due to lower entry-level salaries and an existing wealth of women in the field, men are less likely to begin their careers at a nonprofit leaving the lion's share of these positions to women. Women are also drawn to work at a nonprofit for value-related reasons. Decision making in the nonprofit world tends to be more collaborative than competitive and thus egos and posturing are less likely to be on display as a valued professional trait. Finally, the lower pay of nonprofit work is less discouraging to many women entering the industry who are willing to trade immediate earnings for a greater sense of accomplishment, philanthropy, or social consciousness. Earnings are also less of an issue for women coming back from long stretches of unemployment due to family issues such as stay-at-home motherhood or caring for elderly relatives. Such women take, on average, seven years to return to the workforce and for many of the reasons above the nonprofit sector is a natural first step back.

With the picture of women's involvement in the nonprofit sector becoming clearer, the question now is, "What can women do to break through the nonprofit glass ceiling into leadership positions?" The next section of this report offers insight into the steps that women can take to overcome the various hurdles in nonprofit employment that may prevent movement into leadership or executive positions. It also proposes several changes which can be made at the organizational level to alleviate the lack of female leadership in moderate to large organizations. These barriers not only prevent progress for the women, but also hinder the organizations that deprive women of a fair chance to be on the board and in the driver's seat.

Whether you are a woman considering a career in the nonprofit sector or you already have an established presence in the industry, this report has compiled suggestions from various sources aimed at fast-tracking your rise through the ranks and into leadership and executive positions in line with your career priorities and ambition. As with any career, ambition is paramount to success and therefore is a good place to begin.

Section II:

Bridging the Ambition Gap

and

Setting a Manageable Goal

The Great (Nonprofit) Divide

Current research into women in nonprofit organizations suggests that there is an emerging "ambition gap" among women in low and mid-level employment positions at nonprofits. This gap is simultaneously generational and an issue of perceptions and assumptions made by women in the field.

Women already working for a nonprofit are more or less likely to push for advancement and pay increases based on their age, with older women being the most likely to make such requests. While this may seem to be simply an issue of greater experience and professional acumen providing the confidence to push for advancement, the research suggests that it is not necessarily related to these factors. Rather, the important variable is simply the age of the individual. This is termed the "generational gap," which is a component of the larger "achievement gap."

Competing explanations for the generational gap tend to fall into two camps. The first describes the gap as a result of internalized ambition in older generations of women who have had to fight against even more extreme forms of sexism or exclusionary practices in the past and therefore are more willing to advocate for themselves in the workplace. By highlighting their contributions and worth to the organization and pushing for increases in pay and advancement through the ranks these women are simultaneously the most likely to receive raises and promotions and the

11

most likely to encounter the glass ceiling of their organization. In this way their struggle is a matter of a necessary system change, a topic we will deal with later.

On the other side of the generational gap are younger women who are just beginning to establish their career in the nonprofit world. These women do not yet have the critical experience necessary for top positions and according to research are also less driven to presently want such positions or include them in their long-term plans. Again, this may seem a logical conclusion; to temper your ambitions until they are in line with your experience and confidence within an organization or with a specific population or problem. However, the concern is that when faced with the inevitable hurdles to advancement in medium and large-scale organizations, the ambition and confidence which should arise with time will be harmed by the idea that there is an immovable force preventing their success. Once this idea is internalized, ambition seems to bring only disappointment. Younger generations of women in nonprofit organizations must be willing to make changes to avoid this disappointment and refocus their energy toward positive progress in their careers. This issue is made even more complicated by the fact that emerging research suggests that the millennials, the generation most recently entering the workforce, are more inclined to align their career goals and objectives with a particular cause than to concern themselves with loyalty to their current organization. More than any previous generation they are willing to move to different organizations multiple times due to ideological or philosophical goals, giving little consideration to the impact that such moves may have on their ability to move up the ladder into leadership positions.

This brings us to the first, and perhaps most important lesson; YOU HAVE TO WANT IT! Having the drive, and, most importantly, making it abundantly clear that you are driven to lead your organization is key to bridging the ambition gap. This ambition will separate you from the rank and file and over time will raise the confidence that upper management has in both the ideas and contributions present in your current work and your potential as a leader for the organization as your career develops. This ambition opens the door for involvement in organizational projects and potential mentorship with existing leaders that would otherwise be unavailable to the unambitious. These steps increase your exposure to formal and informal pathways to advancement, making every success you experience yet another demonstration of your ability to work for the organization's mission and lead by example. As important as it is to establish this pattern of ambition and self-promotion, it is equally important to maintain it as habit. This is the first of many times in this short work that we will tiptoe around the classic prescription of "learn to play the game like a man," but research shows that men who boast more about their accomplishments are more likely to be chosen for leadership positions over women. Perhaps it is time for women to do a bit of this 'chest-pounding' as well.

Prescribing these larger behaviors of self-promotion, ambition, and (reasonable) chest-pounding has the benefit of being able to discuss and address the somewhat lofty issues of embedded pathways to advancement and the burden of sexism in the workplace. However, there must ultimately be tangible steps that can be taken every day in order to demonstrate your potential and advocate for yourself as a future leader. As with any journey, it helps to know the destination. The following activity should will help to clarify your personal destination.

Setting Your Goals

Before we begin this section we want you to write your career goal in the space below (Feel free to dream big, but be honest about your ambition):

_____

_____

_____

_____

_____

Naturally, as an ambitious individual, you are no stranger to setting goals. Whether long-term or immediate, professional life is all about working toward your goals. However, when it comes to the larger context of our lives, our life's work, and our careers, we often create goals that, while noble and poetic, are unrealistic, impractical, or unattainable. In the nonprofit world, perhaps the greatest example of such a goal is a person wanting to 'change the world'. In fact, regardless of profession it is likely safe to say that most people have at one time or another been driven by either this or a similarly enormous goal.

The problems that arise from goals of intangible greatness however are endless. Where do you start? How do you know you're on the right track? How will you know when you've succeeded? In order to avoid these pitfalls, numerous methods of goal setting have been proposed for a myriad of settings and personal styles. For our purposes, and simply based on personal preferences and experiences, we focus on creating SMART goals. This particular method emphasizes forming your personal or professional goals by asking, are your goals Specific, Measurable, Achievable, Realistic, and Time-bound? Since you've already established the overarching goal for your career in the space above, use the following table to examine this goal more closely.

SMART	What it means.	Your Goal – How is it SMART?
Specific	Ask yourself: What do you want to accomplish? Why is the goal important? Who is involved in achieving the goal? Where can the goal be attained? Which requirements or restrictions are involved?	
Measurable	Ask yourself: How will I know when I've accomplished my goal? How much? How Many? Focus on quantifiable measures and checkpoints.	
Achievable	Ask yourself: Can YOU achieve the goal? Is it in line with other priorities? Do you have an accurate picture of what it takes to succeed?	
Realistic	Ask yourself: Are there any unavoidable barriers to success? Will your personal background or external factors hurt your efforts?	
Time-Bound	Ask yourself: When do you want to succeed? What can you do today? What can you do in six weeks? Six months?	

Now that you've had a chance to adjust your goal through the SMART process, write your revised goal below:

_____

_____

_____

_____

_____

The goal of this exercise is two-fold. First, while it may seem obvious that anyone who would read this report would be at least marginally driven to advance to a leadership position, the process of laying out your goals and then making them more real by going through some analytical process will often temper the grandeur of your ambition. When faced with some stark realities, many people realize that their true goals are dramatically different from their idealized ambitions. In this case, the suggestions within this report can be taken in parts and with varying levels of intensity based on your newly refined goals. The second purpose, for those who are truly driven to management and leadership positions in their current fields, is to lay out a goal in a way that provides a roadmap for success. By ensuring that your goal is not only SMART but also readily answers the questions that make up each component of a SMART goal, you have in essence laid out the basic steps that must be taken to succeed.

Part III:

5 Steps to Climb the Ladder

Step I: Connect with the Board.

Leadership roles, especially positions hired directly by the board of directors, are typically subject to two competing systems. Boards will often spend a great deal of time developing elaborate profiles for executive and leadership positions within the organization. These profiles detail not only specific job duties and more mundane requirements such as education and experience, but more general characteristics of their "ideal" candidate for the position. Unfortunately, for a great number of organizations these profiles become meaningless when the board decides to hire someone that they have personal relationships with or existing employees that the board simply likes more than other candidates. In these cases the board uses its informal networks to fill the position, likely out of sheer convenience.

For decades men have held a monopoly on such networks to help them with advancement into leadership positions. Because these networks are easily engrained into the workings of a board (they make the selection process easier), involvement in this process can be of great benefit to women who want to advance in their careers. Therefore it is very important to connect with the board if at all possible. Specific actions you can take include:

- Attend open meetings and contribute to relevant discussions.

- Volunteer to present or head projects that the board is interested in.
- Get to know board members in an appropriate personal capacity if possible.
- Find out what other professional or charitable organizations board members are involved in that have relevant activities or volunteer opportunities available.

Simply having one board member who is familiar with your work for the organization and who knows your name can be the difference between consideration for a promotion to a leadership position and waiting another year or two for a position to open.

Step II: Do Your Job

Ha. Actually this tip should read closer to FULFILL YOUR JOB DESCRIPTION, but you get the drift. It is not unheard of in the nonprofit world for employees to take on responsibilities outside of the letter of their job description or, on the flip side, have obsolete or redundant duties in their job description simply because it hasn't been updated in a while. Often through agency growth or shifts in priorities these documents can become outdated when they should be treated as a living document for all positions. It is therefore useful for you to begin to pay closer attention to the actual job you were hired to do. If your job description is wildly inaccurate, or in the case of smaller organizations vague or absent altogether, ask that it be developed or updated to include all of the tasks that you regularly perform but are missing from the document. It can be helpful to create an outline or rough sketch of your position to present to your supervisor prior to initiating this process. Be sure to compare your job as you have framed it to any organizational chart or matrix to prevent creating redundancy or overstepping the duties of your current role. When undertaking this process it is vital to keep the following elements in mind:

1) **Accuracy**. Ensure that any specific tasks are described accurately, keeping in mind any related tasks that may seem superfluous but are involved in accomplishing the task at hand. A good example of this is proficiency in any specific computer program or technology necessary for task completion.

2) **Order**. Be sure to order tasks related to functional or relational responsibilities by importance and frequency. If you are a team leader but occasionally lead department-wide meetings, your immediate priority is at the team level.

3) **Organizational Structure**. Be sure to include information relevant to your position's interplay within the organization. Describe how your work feeds from and into the larger organizational matrix.

4) **Language**. Use straightforward language in the present tense, omitting unnecessary articles, adverbs, or adjectives. Include explanatory phrases when necessary for clarity, but avoid anything which may show bias such as gender specific pronouns where a he/she approach is more appropriate.

By following these guidelines you will be creating a draft document which can be more readily adopted by your supervisors without an overly involved editorial process. As you are the one asking for the review, saving time and energy in the process can make it go much more smoothly.

Below are two job descriptions we came across during our research. They are both for very similar positions at social service nonprofits. The first is an example of a vague, poorly developed job description.

Social Worker

Job Responsibilities:
Help clients by assessing their situation; setting goals; obtaining required services.

Social Worker Job Duties:

- Determines nature of client's situation by interviewing client; assessing medical, psychological, emotional, and social information; making on-site visits.

- Establishes course of action by exploring options; setting goals with client.

- Obtains assistance for client by referring him/her to community resources; arranging for appointments; establishing rapport with other agencies.

- Fosters client's action or adjustment by interpreting attitudes and patterns of behavior; explaining and pointing out new options.

- Maintains record of case by documenting client's situation and client's own actions.

- Monitors planned actions by periodic follow-up.

- Maintains operations by following policies and procedures; participating in quality reviews; reporting needed changes.

- Complies with federal, state, and local legal requirements by studying existing and new legislation; enforcing adherence to requirements; advising management on needed actions.

- Maintains client confidence and protects operations by keeping information confidential.

- Contributes to team effort by accomplishing related results as needed.

Social Worker Skills and Qualifications:
Handles Pressure, Objectivity, Confidentiality, Organization, Planning, Reporting Skills, Persistence, Proactive, Listening, Verbal Communication, Client Relationships

As you can see, the above job description not only does not address a single job duty with any degree of specificity, it includes no references to larger organizational structure, required technical knowledge, or even required educational or professional credentials for holding the position. In contrast, the following job description is a wonderful example of what you would develop using the methods we have discussed.

Social Service Coordinator

GENERAL STATEMENT OF DUTIES: Provides social work skills to assist the resident in attaining or maintaining the highest practicable physical, mental, emotional, and psycho-social well-being.

DISTINGUISHING FEATURES OF THE CLASS: The Social Worker is responsible for assisting residents and families in orientation to (Organization) - its policies and procedures - and to resident rights; assesses and addresses psycho-social needs; advocates for residents. Must possess the ability to make independent decisions when circumstances warrant it. Social workers must possess working knowledge of medical terminology.

EXAMPLES OF WORK:

*Completes comprehensive resident assessment Minimum Data Set (MDS) and Resident Assessment Protocol (RAPS), analyzes and develops comprehensive, individualized care plans for each resident. *The social worker establishes goals for each resident based on mood, behavior, and psycho-social assessment, observation, and interactions;

*Participates in interdisciplinary care planning meetings;

*Documents on chart as mandated by Department of Health regulations, addressing residents' progress toward goals, significant changes, and potential/plan for discharge;

*Is responsible for facilitating discharge process including the completion of a home evaluation, and continually evaluating residents who do not require nursing home level of care;

*Practices supportive intervention; counseling with residents in reaching conflict resolution; provides education to residents;

23

*Advocates for residents by accessing community resources, making referrals to other agencies; consults with in-house resources (psychology and psychiatry);

*Provides resident service;

*Conducts pre-admission visits (when required) and develops social history;

*Maintains regular resident and family contact; greets resident, family members and responsible party on admission day;

*Works together with the interdisciplinary team, incorporates team input/feedback into decision making process;

*Facilitates facility support groups;

*Assists in coordination and organization of psychological and psychiatric services;

*Assists supervisor with planning, developing, organizing, and implementing events;

*Performs other related duties as assigned by supervisor.

*Have ability to manage stress tolerance, pressure and anxiety.

JOB REQUIREMENTS

DESIRED KNOWLEDGE, SKILLS AND ABILITIES: Knowledge of the professional principles and skills used in the practice of Social Work; professional empathy in dealing with residents and families; sense of professional identity while collaborating with co-workers; awareness of community resources and programs for the disabled and elderly; appropriate professional judgment, courtesy and tact.

REQUIRED EDUCATION: B.S.W. or B.A./B.S. in social work or a related field with appropriate college practicum.

As a whole, the process of updating your job description can have several benefits. First of all, if you were hired to perform a list of duties and that list has doubled over the years but your pay has stayed the same, updating the document can help you make the case for an immediate increase in pay commensurate with your current duties. Secondly, it allows you to have a say in how your job is framed within the organization, provided that you are asked to be involved in the process of updating, as you should be. Finally, requesting an update of your job description will make it clear to your supervisors that you are focused on the bigger picture. It sets you apart as a person who wants her place in the agency to be relevant and in line with the organization's mission on a daily basis. It allows you to demonstrate your impact on the success of the agency by aligning your work with its mission and vision in addition to the current expectations and priorities of your organization's leadership.

Step III: Lead from Within Your Current Position

Now that you've established yourself as someone who sees the big picture and is agency-oriented, it's time to demonstrate your ability to lead even before you've been given leadership responsibilities. More commonly this has been called giving yourself the promotion you deserve. There are several components to leading from within your current position. The first is to work to facilitate and improve communication among other employees at your level toward the goal of creating cohesion and unity in agency's mission. One of the most common concerns or complaints in the nonprofit sector, especially within larger organizations, is that the interplay between departments or individuals often becomes fragmented or routinized to the point that people stop seeing themselves as contributing to the greater good that the organization is serving. Since you're already focused on the bigger picture, work to bring these constituent parts of your team together with your enthusiasm. Something as simple as establishing an informal meeting once a week or the creation of an email chain to streamline the communication between and within departments can break up the routine and remind everyone that they serve a vital role. By being proactive you are again reminding the higher-ups that you have the talent to lead while potentially preventing the kinds of communication breakdowns that create the need for reactive solutions to agency problems. These solutions are costly both in terms of time and money, things which are typically in short supply in the nonprofit sector.

It is at this point appropriate to include in this section something of a cautionary note. While the above suggestions can help set you apart from the pack as a leader, it is vital that your supervisors and agency leadership are involved in this process as well, so you do not appear to go over the head of your superiors or overstep your existing role within the agency. Unfortunately, unchecked ambition, especially when it might threaten the current state of affairs which some rely on, may be perceived as arrogance or at least aggressive posturing in the workplace. Be sure to make it clear that you are simply forging your own path to leadership, not trying to hijack someone else's.

Step IV: Become your agency's go-to-gal.

In addition to attending relevant board meetings, involve yourself in your agency's mission outside of the office. Go to conferences relevant to your work to familiarize yourself with industry trends, changes, and developments. Attend workshops that can help you become more efficient in your work, and advocate for the things you learn to be implemented as standard practice, so long as you can clearly demonstrate the benefit of these changes to management. Join professional organizations and read industry publications related to not only your specific job function but the nonprofit sector and your client population in general. Stay abreast of the latest research in program development and implementation, management, and any other element of your current work and the work you want to move into. For women in older generations, learn to utilize new technologies and social media to connect with peers and access information to stay current and relevant in your field. By simply increasing your working knowledge of your chosen field and the sector as a whole you can set yourself above those who are concerned only with their current job and its duties. This is valuable when it comes time to fill an open leadership position.

This kind of outside interest in your work is natural in social services and nonprofit work anyway, being a field driven by passion and desire to help your fellow human beings, so why not make the extra effort and turn that inherent interest into something you can put on your resume? Now I understand that this can be a slippery slope suggestion, where the end result is a complete imbalance in your work / life mix, however most organizations see the benefit in this kind of activity and will likely accommodate a reasonable amount of this as part of your employment. While they probably won't fly you out to a weeklong conference on homelessness, they likely won't take issue with you attending a few local meetings a month during business hours. Such involvement in the field has the added benefit of becoming the de-facto face of your organization at these events, a role that anyone seeking leadership should embrace actively.

Step V: Change the System

We hate to begin this section with a sports metaphor but this is one that we feel is especially poignant given recent research. There's a saying in ALL men's sports; "That's why girls don't play the game." Now this phrase is used in any situation where the difficulty, pain, violence, or sheer "male-ness" of the game is put on display all at one moment. A quarterback is sacked hard and loses consciousness for a minute, a baseball player takes an inside pitch to the ribcage, or a hockey player is knocked out getting checked in open ice; that's why girls don't play the game. (To be clear, we consider this not only sexist, but untrue in terms of the ability of women to play hard and absorb bone-crushing blows in any sport.)

For decades the huge majority of what were considered legitimate employment opportunities worked with the same, albeit unwritten, rule. Leadership, management, and the rigor of the corporate world were the sole realms of men. They wrote the rules and therefore were really the only one's capable of playing the game as it was meant to be played. Thankfully, time and social struggle has done much to remedy this state of affairs, however the need for change at the structural level still exists if we are ever going to rewrite the rules to give women an equal chance at success.

What we have currently in the employment world strongly mimics the state of sports. We have parallel sports leagues for women and men, but clearly emphasize the importance of male athletic endeavors over their female counterparts. This kind of 'separate but equal' implementation does little to promote equal access or change the larger perceptions that allow gender disparity to continue unabated. Moreover, many of the recommended changes to these systems are simply lip-service in the face of criticism that will most likely blow over given enough time. In fact, given recent trends, a new study by the University of Denver and the White House Project suggest that women will reach parity with men in nonprofit leadership positions sometime around 2085 – that's 70 years from now!

This prediction will only come true of course, if we continue to play by the rules as they have been laid out before us. We must foster a culture that empowers women in their search for leadership position in the same way it does men. The first step in this complicated process is to actively support the training and advancement of women into leadership roles. It must be established as a goal of organizations to not only find the best and brightest of both sexes to fill open positions, but to provide women with the same kind of mentoring and professional advancement programs that have been available to men for ages. We must also ensure that these processes are formalized in an attempt to overcome the informal

29

networks and pathways to advancement that we have already discussed. It is not enough to simply tell women to learn the rules of the game and play them more like a man might, we must guarantee that the game itself CAN be played in such a manner. It is essential to create an environment where healthy communication and relationships are allowed to grow and feed the culture and success of each organization without excluding, whether on purpose or not, any one group of employees.

A major part of this culture should be to address the presence of different value systems, especially between gender groups. Organizations have to be sensitive to the work / family balancing act that many women in the nonprofit sector are subject to, or may have to deal with as they expand their families in the future. They must be willing to look at professional leave requests or prior gaps in employment in terms of this value dynamism and not solely through the lens of historical or traditional ideas of professionalism, acumen, or dedication to a cause. Finally, organizations must involve women in the process of change and implementation that will accompany each component part of the shift in the way we approach women in leadership roles. One of the biggest keys to retaining women with the highest levels of education and experience is to make this entire process of change inclusive in order to build these elements into the workplace culture where they may have a legitimate chance of taking root for future growth. This involvement creates ownership and a sense of responsibility for the success of these changes and the results will be far superior to policies thought up and implemented in a boardroom without significant input from those "in the trenches."

What this means for women currently holding or seeking leadership roles is that they must be committed to change not only for themselves but for fellow women in the field now and in the future. The old camping adage, "leave it better than you found it" should suffice here. Enjoy the success you have found, once you have found it of course, but always be mindful that you are in essence a pioneer in a new territory and conduct yourself accordingly. Fight to make changes that help improve access for each new generation of future female nonprofit leaders and, hopefully, you will help to beat the woeful 2085 forecast by a few decades.

If we may, in conclusion, continue with the sports metaphor with which we began… One of the biggest hurdles to the legitimacy of this short work, as we saw it upon undertaking the project, was to avoid coming off as advocating that women simply take on a more masculine approach to their careers in the nonprofit world, vis-à-vis leadership roles. To do so would be the same as telling a professional female basketball player to play more like a man and assume she could make it in the NBA. This would ignore the dramatic differences in the way that the same sport is played by two distinctly different groups. Women and men *often* possess different skill sets, values, priorities, and foundations for the execution of their professional duties. Neither one has more intrinsic value than the other, but they are often distinctive and may not fit the predefined approaches of our existing notions of success, efficacy, or the "right (wo)man for the job." These are all larger issues than we are prepared to tackle here.

We are however reminded of Jennie Finch. Ms. Finch is a former All-American softball pitcher who led the US Olympic team to gold and silver medals in 2004 and 2008 respectively, and has been called the greatest softball pitcher of her era. In addition to her unquestionable proficiency on the mound, she was also the only female athlete in People Magazine's 2004 "50 Most Beautiful People," modeled for Sports Illustrated, and was a co-host on This Week in Baseball, a syndicated network baseball program. In her role as a co-host she would regularly pitch against active Major League Baseball players, often striking them out. She was so good at picking apart batters that several big name hitters outright refused to face her out of fear of embarrassment. In 2004 she struck out Albert Pujols, Mike Piazza, and Brian Giles at an All-Star Softball game. (All three men are among the top hitters to ever play the game of baseball.) The reason that she was so feared by baseball players and so successful against them wasn't that she threw harder or faster than the pitchers they were used to facing, it was simply that she used her skills to show them pitches they had never seen before. Were she to try and pitch like a man, or even adapt her skills to the game of baseball, she would have likely met with failure. Instead she embraced the talents she developed playing the game of softball and understood how to apply them when facing a baseball player.

Examples of this type of skill repurposing are endless, especially in sports, and it is important to take away from such stories the idea that every experience we have and every skill we develop can be utilized toward our own specific goals. For women who want to succeed in the nonprofit sector and land a leadership position from which they might do great good in the world, the empathy they developed as a mother, the understanding they honed as a spouse, and the patience they have developed from years if not decades of struggle against systems that are not inclined toward their success will all serve them well as leaders in any field. They must only be willing to take the steps.

✓ Connect with the Board.

✓ Do your Job.

✓ Lead from within your Current Position.

✓ Become Your Agency's Go-to-Gal.

✓ Change the System.

Part IV

Wrapping Up

A Word on Social Entrepreneurship

While women are dramatically under-represented in leadership roles at the largest nonprofit organizations, there is another field where women are doing quite well while following their passion for traditionally nonprofit causes. Among social entrepreneurs, females are dramatically outperforming their male counterparts. In fact, in two separate rankings of social entrepreneurs taken in 2009 and 2011, 7 of the top 10 most successful were found to be women. Additionally, among social capital firms which support such socially responsible entrepreneurship, 6 of the top 10 were led by women. Overall, women make up roughly 60% of all social entrepreneurs at present. While they are not strictly confined to the nonprofit sector, the increased emphasis on accountability among nonprofits and the need for innovative solutions to persistent social problems has made the social entrepreneur an indispensable part of the future of social welfare organizations.

Women appear to be especially talented at taking on this role. Several explanations have been advanced to explain how women have dominated the ranks of this new kind of business leader; however the one which is most recurrent is that the absence of traditional gatekeepers makes taking on the role of innovator equally possible for men and women. When given truly equal access to real leadership roles, women are simply outperforming men.

35

The point of this is to lay out an alternative pathway for women in the nonprofit sector. While the landscape of the traditional nonprofit is no doubt changing, albeit slowly in many cases, there has been arguably no better time than the present to invest in your own passion for your work and push for innovation outside of the traditional confines of the nonprofit sector. Of course, we are not suggesting that you immediately quit your job and strike out on your own, but rather that you examine how you can use the experience you have gained to propose new solutions, paradigms, or an entirely new methodology to your work. Many successful, socially responsible organizations have been created in spare time, with novel solutions to any number of problems. In much the same spirit that we previously proposed 'giving' yourself the promotion you deserve, sometimes, in the face of organizational gridlock or systemic barriers, the best step is one outside of the box.

Conclusion

While this work is by no means an exhaustive collection of the endless material out there aimed at helping women succeed in business, it is our hope that it is able to do something that much of the business self-help genre does not do well, provide a succinct overview of actionable steps that can be taken immediately without the need for psychologizing the issue or making your personal advancement within your organization about much larger social or political issues. Clearly there is need for reform in most corners of our society where gender is concerned, but outside of the extremes of revolution, these changes will likely take much more time than you, as a driven, career-oriented, female future-leader of a nonprofit have to spare. Furthermore, we hope that the limited discussion of these larger issues which has been included has demystified the challenges you will face along the way. While no single work contains the Holy Grail of success, we can assure you that if you put into practice the steps described herein you will set yourself apart in your organization as someone who is driven to lead. The road may be longer for some, but for the dedicated and persistent success is the inevitable destination. Good Luck!

Select References

The Untapped Potential of Women in Nonprofits. The Chronical of Philanthropy. April 28, 2014

Benchmarking Women's Leadership in the United States. University of Denver, Colorado Women's College, The White House Project. 2012

Women Leaders and Work from a Nonprofit Perspective. Tensie Whelan. May 15, 2013, Huffington Post.

Are Women Underrepresented as Leaders of Nonprofit Organizations? Joan E. Pynes. University of South Florida. Review of Public Personnel Administration. April 20, 2000.

Women and Power in the Nonprofit Sector. Teresa Jean Odendahl & Michael O'Neill. Jossey-Bass, 1994.

Additional Written Resources

If you've found the information in this report intriguing, be sure to look carefully at the next pages to find out more about CAN-DO and what some of CAN-DO's other information products are. Every book, report and video address one or more ways you can bring new ideas to your organization, improve skills, build knowledge and solve problems. You owe it to yourself to sign up at no cost on the email list to receive notifications on the latest products that will help you lead a better organization. Go to www.uta.edu/can-do to sign up now. When you do this, you'll gain access to a valuable exclusive report, available for free ONLY to CAN-DO subscribers.

Can We Do Something More for You?

CAN-DO! The Center for Advocacy, Nonprofit and Donor Organizations [CAN-DO] is the nonprofit research and capacity-building arm of the School of Social Work, University of Texas at Arlington. We are committed to working with nonprofits to help achieve higher levels of excellence and positive client outcomes.

We are self-supporting through developing mutually beneficial contracts with our nonprofit organizational clients. Initial consultations are always free and we work diligently to keep your investments in our services as low as possible.

For your free consultation, contact Dr. Rick Hoefer by email at rhoefer@uta.edu to begin a conversation about increasing the capacity and visibility of your organization. Dr. Hoefer is the Roy E. Dulak Professor for Community Practice Research at the School of Social Work at the University of Texas at Arlington. He directs the Center for Advocacy, Nonprofit and Donor Organizations (CAN-DO).

Dr. Hoefer specializes in translating cutting edge, best practice research into usable practice points for organizations. His passion is helping nonprofits succeed in providing high quality services to our communities. He has over 25 years of experience working in and with nonprofit organizations, assisting them in improving their services through program evaluation, advocacy, and management consulting. Dr. Hoefer has authored more than 30 published journal articles and 6 books and has given scores of presentations in the fields of nonprofit management, advocacy, program evaluation and policy practice.

John Yowell is a former educator and current graduate student in Social Work and Sociology with research experience in Family and Gender Sociology, Critical Theory, and Nonprofit Management. He can be reached at JMYowell@gmail.com.

www.ingramcontent.com/pod-product-compliance
Lightning Source LLC
Chambersburg PA
CBHW071018180526
45168CB00003B/1473